THE
DEEPER
LIFE

D0839207

THE DEEPER LIFE

Robert Murray McCheyne

Edited with an Introduction by
Lyle W. Dorsett and David P. Setran

World Wide Publications

The Deeper Life
by Robert Murray McCheyne
Introduction © 1994 Lyle W. Dorsett and David P. Setran
Cover and typesetting © 1994
Billy Graham Evangelistic Association

Published by World Wide Publications 1994
in cooperation with the Institute of Evangelism,
Billy Graham Center, Wheaton, IL.

ISBN: 0-89066-248-7
Printed in the United States of America

Contents

Introduction

Robert Murray McCheyne was only twenty-nine years old when he died. Despite the brevity of his life, his profound impact for Christ Jesus and His kingdom continues a century and a half later.

McCheyne was born in Edinburgh, Scotland, on May 21, 1813. Although he was raised in a faithful Church of Scotland family, he never experienced the regenerating touch of Christ's Spirit until he was eighteen. Grief over the death of an older brother in 1831 was the impetus for McCheyne's spiritual conversion—a transformation that manifested itself in the confession of sins, sincere repentance, and a deep sense of calling into full-time pastoral and evangelistic ministry.

After studying theology and church history at the University of Edinburgh, McCheyne was ordained in the Church of Scotland. Although the young pastor had only seven and a half years to minister before he died, his sojourn reveals that the quality of a life, rather than its length, is the key to success. During his short pilgrimage, the Reverend McCheyne, pastor of St. Peter's Church, Dundee, led many souls to Christ Jesus and helped countless others know the Lord better and love Him more.

His own life was a striking example of personal holiness. A close associate said of him, "Whether viewed as a son, a brother, friend, or a pastor, often has the remark been made by those who knew him most intimately, that he was the most faultless and attractive exhibition of the true Christian which they had ever seen embodied in a living form."[1] McCheyne spent a good deal of his time, both personally and in his preaching, studying the disciplines of the Christ-like life. He arose well before the dawn to take time for prayer and Bible reading. His great goal was to be in Christ before being in ministry, allowing his service to be a simple outflow of the cultivation of his spirit within. Of him it was said, "The real secret of his soul's prosperity lay in the daily enlargement of his heart and fellowship with his God. And the river deepened as it flowed on to eternity."[2]

Besides his considerable evangelistic and pastoral ministry, McCheyne continues to help people grow in Christ through his written work, most of which was published and edited posthumously by Andrew A. Bonar in three volumes: *Memoir and Remains of the Reverend Robert Murray McCheyne* (1844), *Additional Remains of Robert Murray McCheyne* (1846), and *A Basket of Fragments* (1848).

The following pages are comprised of excerpts from McCheyne's letters, addresses, sermons, and journals. These devotional nuggets have been edifying Christians for over one hundred and fifty years. Equally important is the Bible calendar reprinted at the end of this book. Originally prepared by McCheyne in 1842 for his congregation in Dundee, it is still being widely used all over the world. McCheyne was prompted to arrange this calendar and make it available to his congregation because he knew that many of them had never read the entire

Bible. Furthermore, few members of his flock fed daily on God's inspired message. Recognizing that prescribed readings can lead to dead formality, self-righteousness, carelessness, or even a "yoke too heavy to bear," he nevertheless advocated consuming this "daily bread," despite the dangers, because an enormous blessing awaits those who undertake the discipline in a proper spirit. Among the advantages McCheyne noted are these:

1. "The entire Bible will be read through in an orderly manner in the course of a year—the Old Testament once, the New Testament and Psalms twice."

2. "Time will not be wanted in choosing portions to read."

3. ". . . all [who join you in this endeavor will] be feeding in the same portion of this green pasture at the same time."[3]

Lyle W. Dorsett
David P. Setran
Wheaton, Illinois, 1994

Note: The excerpts that follow have been taken from the writings of Andrew Bonar, both in his *Memoir and Remains of the Reverend Robert Murray McCheyne* (1881 ed.) and the subsequent *Additional Remains of Robert Murray McCheyne* (1881 ed.).

1

Personal Renewal

Personal Reformation.

I am persuaded that I shall obtain the highest amount of present happiness, I shall do most for God's glory and the good of man, and I shall have the fullest reward in eternity, by maintaining a conscience always washed in Christ's blood, by being filled with the Holy Spirit at all times, and by attaining the most entire likeness to Christ in mind, will, and heart, that is possible for a redeemed sinner to attain to in this world.

I am persuaded that whenever any one from without, or my own heart from within, at any moment, or in any circumstances, contradicts this—if anyone shall insinuate that it is not for my present and eternal happiness, and for God's glory and my usefulness, to maintain a blood-washed conscience, to be entirely filled with the Spirit, and to be fully conformed to the image of Christ in all things—that is the voice of the devil, God's enemy, the enemy of my soul and of all good—the most foolish, wicked, and miserable of all the creatures. See Prov. ix.17: "Stolen waters are sweet."

1. *To maintain a conscience void of offense,* I am persuaded that I ought to confess my sins more. I think I ought to confess sin the moment I see it to be sin; whether I am in company, or in study, or even preaching, the soul ought to cast a glance of abhorrence at the sin. If I go on with the duty, leaving the sin unconfessed, I go on with a burdened conscience, and add sin to sin. I think I ought at certain times of the day—my best times—say, after breakfast and after tea—to confess solemnly the sins of the previous hours, and to seek their complete remission.

I find that the devil often makes use of the confession of sin to stir up again the very sin confessed into new exercise, so that I am afraid to dwell upon the confession. I must ask experienced Christians about this. For the present, I think I should strive against this awful abuse of confession, whereby the devil seeks to frighten me away from confessing. I ought to take all methods for seeing the vileness of my sins. I ought to regard myself as a condemned branch of Adam—as partaker of a nature opposite to God from the womb (Ps. li.)—as having a heart full of all wickedness, which pollutes every thought, word, and action, during my whole life, from birth to death.

I ought to confess often the sins of my youth, like David and Paul—my sins before conversion—my sins since conversion—sins against light and knowledge, against love and grace, against each person of the Godhead. I ought to look at my sins in the light of the holy law, in the light of God's countenance, in the light of the cross, in the light of the judgment-seat, in the light of hell, in the light of eternity. I ought to examine my dreams, my floating thoughts, my predilections, my often recurring actions, my habits of thought, feeling, speech, and action—the slanders of my enemies, and the reproofs, and even banterings, of my friends—to find out traces of my prevailing sin, matter for confession.

I ought to have a stated day of confession, with fasting—say, once a month. I ought to have a number of scriptures marked, to bring sin to remembrance. I ought to make use of all bodily affliction, domestic trial, frowns of providence on myself, house, parish, church, or country, as calls from God to confess sin. The sins and afflictions of other men should call me to the same.

I ought, on Sabbath evenings, and on communion Sabbath evenings, to be especially careful to confess the sins of holy things. I ought to confess the sins of my confessions—their imperfections, sinful aims, self-righteous tendency, etc.—and to look to Christ as having confessed my sins perfectly over His own sacrifice.

I ought to go to Christ for the forgiveness of each sin. In washing my body, I go over every spot, and wash it out. Should I be less careful in washing my soul? I ought to see the stripe that was made on the back of Jesus by each of my sins. I ought to see the infinite pang thrill through the soul of Jesus equal to an eternity of my hell for my sins, and for all of them. I ought to see that in Christ's bloodshedding there is an infinite over-payment for all my sins. Although Christ did not suffer more than infinite justice demanded, yet He could not suffer at all without laying down an infinite ransom.

I feel, when I have sinned, an immediate reluctance to go to Christ. I am ashamed to go. I feel as if it would do no good to go—as if it were making Christ a minister of sin, to go straight from the swine-trough to the best robe—and a thousand other excuses; but I am persuaded they are all lies, direct from hell. John argues the opposite way: "If any man sin, we have an advocate with the Father"; (1 Jn. 2:1) and a thousand other scriptures are against it. I am sure there is neither peace nor safety from deeper sin, but in going directly to the Lord Jesus Christ. This is God's way of peace and holiness. It is folly to the world and the beclouded heart, but it is *the way*.

I must never think a sin too small to need immediate application to the blood of Christ. If I put away a good conscience, concerning faith I made shipwreck. I must never think my sins too great, too aggravated, too presumptuous—as when done on my knees, or in preaching, or by a dying bed, or during dangerous illness—to hinder me from fleeing to Christ. The weight of my sins should act like the weight of a clock: the heavier it is, it makes it go the faster.

I must not only wash in Christ's blood, but clothe me in Christ's obedience. For every sin of omission in self, I may find a divinely perfect obedience ready for me in Christ. For every sin of commission in self, I may find not only a stripe or a wound in Christ, but also a perfect rendering of the opposite obedience in my place, so that the law is magnified, its curse more than carried, its demand more than answered.

Often the doctrine of *Christ for me* appears common, well known, having nothing new in it; and I am tempted to pass it by and go to some scripture more taking. This is the devil again—a red-hot lie. *Christ for us* is ever new, ever glorious. "Unsearchable riches of Christ"—an infinite object, and the only one for a guilty soul. I ought to have a number of scriptures ready, which lead my blind soul directly to Christ, such as Isaiah xlv., Rom. iii.

2. *To be filled with the Holy Spirit,* I am persuaded that I ought to study more my own weakness. I ought to have a number of scriptures ready to be meditated on, such as Rom. vii., John xv., to convince me that I am a helpless worm.

I am tempted to think that I am now an established Christian, that I have overcome this or that lust so long, that I have got into the habit of the opposite grace, so that there is no fear; I may venture very near the temptation—nearer than other men. This is a lie of Satan. I might as well speak of gunpowder getting by habit a power of resisting fire, so as not to catch the spark. As long as powder is wet, it resists the spark; but when it becomes dry, it is ready to explode at the first touch. As long as the Spirit dwells in my heart, He deadens me to sin, so that, if lawfully called through temptation, I may reckon upon God carrying me through. But when the Spirit leaves me, I am like dry gunpowder. Oh for a sense of this!

I am tempted to think that there are some sins for which I have no natural taste, such as strong drink, profane language, etc., so that I need not fear temptation to such sins. This is a lie, a proud, presumptuous lie. The seeds of all sins are in my heart, and perhaps all the more dangerously that I do not see them.

I ought to pray and labor for the deepest sense of my utter weakness and helplessness that ever a sinner was brought to feel. I am helpless in respect of every lust that ever was, or ever will be, in the human heart. I am a worm, a beast, as if it would not be safe for me to renounce all indwelling strength, as if it would be dangerous for me to feel (what is the truth) that there is nothing in me keeping me back from the grossest and vilest sin. This is a delusion of the devil.

My only safety is to know, feel, and confess my helplessness, that I may hang upon the arm of Omnipotence. . . . I daily wish that sin had been rooted out of my heart. I say, "Why did God leave the root of lasciviousness, pride, anger, etc., in my bosom? He hates sin, and I hate it; why did He not take it clean away?" I know many answers to this which completely satisfy my judgment, but still I do not *feel* satisfied. This is wrong. It is right to be weary of the being of sin, but not right to quarrel with my present 'good fight of faith.'

The falls of professors into sin make me tremble. I have been driven away from prayer, and burdened in a fearful manner by hearing or seeing their sin. This is wrong. It is right to tremble, and to make every sin of every professor a lesson of my own helplessness; but it should lead me the more to Christ . . . If I were more deeply convinced of my utter helplessness, I think I would not be so alarmed when I hear of the falls of other men. I should study those sins in which I am most helpless, in which passion becomes like a whirlwind and I like a straw. No figure of speech can represent my utter want of power to resist the torrent of sin.

I ought to study Christ's omnipotence more: Heb. vii. 25, 1 Thess. v. 23, Rom. vi. 14, Rom. v. 9,10, and such scriptures, should be ever before me. Paul's thorn (2 Cor. xii.) is the experience of the greater part of my life. It should be ever before me. There are many subsidiary methods of seeking deliverance from sins, which must not be neglected— thus, marriage (1 Cor. vii. 2); fleeing (1 Tim. vi. 11; 1 Cor. vi. 18); watch and pray (Matt. xxvi. 41); the word, "It is written, it is written." So Christ defended Himself (Matt. iv.). But the main defense is casting myself into the arms of Christ like a helpless child, and beseeching Him to fill me with the Holy Spirit. "This is the victory that overcometh the world, even our faith" (1 John v. 4,5)—a wonderful passage.

I ought to study Christ as a living Savior more— as a Shepherd, carrying the sheep He finds, as a King, reigning in and over the souls He has redeemed, as a Captain, fighting with those who fight with me (Ps. xxxv.)—as one who has engaged to bring me through all temptations and trials, however impossible to flesh and blood.

I am often tempted to say, How can this Man save us? How can Christ in Heaven deliver me from lusts which I feel raging in me, and nets I feel enclosing me? This is the father of lies again! "He is able to save unto the uttermost."

I ought to study Christ as an Intercessor. He prayed most for Peter, who was to be most tempted. I am on His breastplate. If I could hear Christ praying for me in the next room, I would not fear a million enemies. Yet the distance makes no difference; He is praying for me!

I ought to study the Comforter more—His Godhead, His love, His Almightiness. I have found by experience that nothing sanctifies me so much as meditating on the Comforter, as John xiv. 16. And yet how seldom I do this! Satan keeps me from it. I am often like those men who said, They know not if there be any Holy Ghost. I ought never to forget that my body is dwelt in by the third Person of the Godhead. The very thought of this should make me tremble to sin (1 Cor. vi.). I ought never to forget that sin grieves the Holy Spirit—vexes and quenches Him. If I would be filled with the Spirit, I feel I must read the Bible more, pray more, and watch more.

3. *To gain entire likeness to Christ,* I ought to get a high esteem of the happiness of it. I am persuaded that God's happiness is inseparably linked in with His holiness. Holiness and happiness are like light and heat. God never tasted one of the pleasures of sin.

Christ had a body such as I have, yet He never tasted one of the pleasures of sin. The redeemed, through all eternity, will never taste pleasures of sin; yet their happiness is complete. It would be my greatest happiness to be from this moment entirely like them. Every sin is something away from my greatest enjoyment. The devil strives night and day to make me forget this or disbelieve it. He says, "Why should you not enjoy this pleasure as much as Solomon or David? You may go to heaven also." I am persuaded that this is a lie—my true happiness is to go and sin no more.

I ought not to delay parting with sins. Now is God's time. "I made haste and delayed not." I ought not to spare sins because I have long allowed them as infirmities, and others would think it odd if I were to change all at once. What a wretched delusion of Satan that is!

Whatever I see to be sin, I ought from this hour to set my whole soul against it, using all scriptural methods to mortify it—as the Scriptures, special prayer for the Spirit, fasting, watching.

I ought to mark strictly the occasions when I have fallen, and avoid the occasion as much as the sin itself.

Satan often tempts me to go as near to temptations as possible without committing the sin. This is fearful—tempting God and grieving the Holy Ghost. It is a deep-laid plot of Satan.

I ought to flee all temptation, according to Prov. iv. 15: "Avoid it, pass not by it, turn from it, and pass away." Entire conformity to Christ—for the whole law to be written on my heart—I ought statedly and solemnly to give my heart to God, to surrender my all into His everlasting arms, according to the prayer (Ps. xxxi.), "Into Thine hand I commit my spirit." I ought to beseech Him not to let any iniquity, secret or presumptuous, have dominion over me, and to fill me with every grace that is in Christ, in the highest degree that it is possible for a redeemed sinner to receive it, and at all times, till death.

I ought to meditate often on heaven as a world of holiness, where all are holy, where the joy is holy joy, the work holy work; so that, without personal holiness, I never can be there. I ought to avoid the appearance of evil. God commands me; and I find that Satan has a singular art in linking the appearance and reality together.

I find that speaking of some sins defiles my mind and leads me into temptation. I find that God forbids even saints to speak of the things that are done of them in secret. I ought to avoid this.

Eve, Achan, David, all fell through the lust of the eye. I should make a covenant with mine, and pray, "Turn away mine eyes from viewing vanity." Satan makes unconverted men like the deaf adder to the sound of the Gospel. I should pray to be made deaf by the Holy Spirit to all that would tempt me to sin.

One of my most frequent occasions of being led into temptation is this—I say it is needful to my office that I listen to this, or look into this, or speak of this. So far this is true; yet I am sure Satan has his part in this argument. I should seek divine direction to settle how far it will be good for my ministry, and how far evil for my soul, that I may avoid the latter.

I am persuaded that nothing is thriving in my soul unless it is growing. "Grow in grace." "Lord, increase our faith." "Forgetting the things that are behind." I am persuaded that I ought to be inquiring at God and man what grace I want, and how I may become more like Christ. I ought to strive for more purity, humility, meekness, patience under suffering, love. "Make me Christ-like in all things," should be my constant prayer. "Fill me with the Holy Spirit."

Reformation in Secret Prayer.

I ought not to omit any of the parts of prayer—

confession, adoration, thanksgiving, petition, and intercession.

There is a fearful tendency to omit *confession*, proceeding from low views of God and His law, slight views of my heart and the sins of my past life. This must be resisted. There is a constant tendency to omit *adoration,* when I forget to whom I am speaking, when I rush heedlessly into the presence of Jehovah, without remembering His awful name and character, when I have little eyesight for His glory, and little admiration of His wonders. "Where are the wise?" I have the native tendency of the heart to omit *giving thanks.* And yet it is specially commanded (Phil. iv. 6). Often when the heart is selfish, dead to the salvation of others, I omit *intercession.* And yet it especially is the spirit of the great Advocate, who has the name of Israel always on His heart.

Perhaps every prayer need not have all these; but surely a day should not pass without some space being devoted to each.

I ought to pray before seeing any one. Often when I sleep long, or meet with others early, and then have family prayer, and breakfast, and forenoon callers, often it is eleven or twelve o'clock before I begin secret prayer. This is a wretched system. It is unscriptural. Christ rose before day, and went into a solitary place. David says, "Early will I seek Thee; Thou shalt early hear my voice." Mary Magdalene came to the sepulcher while yet it was dark. Family prayer loses much of its power and sweetness; and I can do no good to those who come to seek from me. The conscience feels guilty, the soul unfed, the lamp not trimmed. Then, when secret prayer comes, the soul is often out of tune. I feel it is far better to begin with God, to see His face first, to get my soul near Him before it is near another. "When I awake I am still with Thee."

If I have slept too long, or am going on an early journey, or my time is any way shortened, it is best to dress hurriedly, and have a few minutes alone with God, than to give it up for lost.

But, in general, it is best to have at least one hour *alone with God,* before engaging in anything else. At the same time, I must be careful not to reckon communion with God by minutes or hours, or by solitude. I have pored over my Bible, and on my knees for hours, with little or no communion; and my times of solitude have been oftentimes of greatest temptation.

As to *intercession,* I ought daily to intercede for my own family, connections, relatives, and friends; also for my flock—the believers, the awakened, the careless; the sick, the bereaved; the poor, the rich; my elders, Sunday-school teachers, day-school teachers, children, tract distributors—that all means may be blessed. Sunday preaching and teaching; visiting of the sick, visiting from house to house; providences, sacraments. I ought daily to intercede briefly for the whole town, the Church of Scotland, all faithful ministers; for vacant congregations, students of divinity, etc.; for dear brethren by name; for missionaries to Jews and Gentiles—and for this end I must read missionary reports regularly, and get acquainted with all that is doing throughout the world. It would stir me up to pray with the map before me. I must have a scheme of prayer, also the names of missionaries marked on the map. I ought to pray at large for the above on Saturday morning and evening from seven to eight. Perhaps also I might take different parts for different days; only I ought daily to plead for my family and flock. I ought to pray in everything. "Be careful for nothing, but in *everything* . . . by prayer and supplication, make your requests known unto God."

Often I receive a letter asking to preach, or some such request. I find myself answering before having asked counsel of God. Still oftener a person calls and asks me something, and I do not ask direction. Often I go out to visit a sick person in a hurry, without asking His blessing, which alone can make the visit of any use. I am persuaded that I ought never to do anything without prayer, and, if possible, special, secret prayer.

In reading the history of the Church of Scotland, I see how much her troubles and trials have been connected with the salvation of souls and the glory of Christ. I ought to pray far more for our Church, for our leading ministers by name, and for my own clear guidance in the right way, that I may not be led aside, or driven aside, from following Christ. Many difficult questions may be forced on us for which I am not fully prepared, such as the lawfulness of covenants. I should pray much more in peaceful days, that I may be guided rightly when days of trial come.

I ought to spend the best hours of the day in communion with God. It is my noblest and most fruitful employment, and is not to be thrust into any corner. The morning hours, from six to eight, are the most uninterrupted, and should be thus employed, if I can prevent drowsiness. A little time after breakfast might be given to intercession. After tea is my best hour, and that should be solemnly dedicated to God if possible.

I ought not to give up the good old habit of prayer before going to bed; but guard must be kept against sleep: planning what things I am to ask is the best remedy. When I awake in the night, I ought to rise and pray, as David and as John Welsh did.

I ought to read three chapters of the Bible in secret every day, at least.

I ought on Sunday morning to look over all the chapters read through the week, and especially the verses marked. I ought to read in three different places; I ought also to read according to subjects, lives, etc.

2

Do What You Can

"She hath done what she could; she is come
aforehand to anoint My body to
the burying."—Mark xiv. 8

Doctrine—Do what you can.

From the Gospel of John (xi. 2), we learn that
this woman was Mary, the sister of Lazarus and
Martha. We have already learned that she was an
eminent believer: "She sat at the feet of Jesus, and
heard His word." Jesus Himself said of her: "Mary
hath chosen the good part, which shall not be taken
away from her." Now it is interesting to see this same
Mary eminent in another way—not only as a *contemplative believer,* but as an *active believer.*

Many seem to think that to be a believer is to
have certain feelings and experiences; forgetting all
the time that these are but the flowers, and that the
fruit must follow. The engrafting of the branch is
good, the inflowing of the sap good, but the fruit is
the end in view. So faith is good, and peace and joy
are good, but holy fruit is the end for which we are
saved.

I trust many of you, last Sunday, were like Mary, sitting at the Redeemer's feet, and hearing His word. Now I would persuade you to be like Mary, in *doing what you can for Christ*. If you have been bought with a price, then glorify God in your body and spirit, which are His. I beseech you by the mercies of God.

These are things which we can do.

1. *We could love Christ, pray and praise more.* What this woman did she did to Christ. Jesus had saved her soul, had saved her brother and sister, and she felt that she could not do too much for Him. She brought an alabaster box of ointment, very costly, and broke the box, and poured it on His head. No doubt she loved His disciples—holy John and frank Peter—yet still she loved Christ more. No doubt she loved Christ's poor, and was often kind to them; yet she loved Jesus more.

On His blessed head, that was so soon to be crowned with thorns—on His blessed feet, that were so soon to be pierced with nails—she poured the precious ointment. This is what we should do. If we have been saved by Christ, we could pour out our best affections on Him. It is well to love His disciples, well to love His ministers, well to love His poor, but it is best to love Himself.

We cannot now reach His blessed head, nor anoint His holy feet; but we can fall down at His footstool, and pour out our affections towards Him. It was not the ointment Jesus cared for—what does the King of Glory care for a little ointment?—but it is the loving heart, poured out upon His feet. It is the adoration, praise, love, and prayers of a believer's broken heart, that Christ cares for. The new heart is the alabaster box that Jesus loves.

Oh, brethren, could you not do more in this way? Could you not give more time to pouring out your heart to Jesus—breaking the box, and filling the room with the odor of your praise? Could you not pray more than you do to be filled with the Spirit, that the Spirit may be poured down on ministers, and God's people, and on an unconverted world? Jesus loves tears and groans from a broken heart.

2. *We could live holier lives.* The Church is thus described in the Song of Solomon: "Who is this that cometh out of the wilderness like pillars of smoke, perfumed with myrrh and frankincense, with all powders of the merchant?" The holiness of the believer is like the most precious perfume. When a holy believer goes through the world, filled with the Spirit, made more than conqueror, the fragrance fills the room; "tis as if an angel shook his wings."

If the world were full of believers, it would be like a bed of spices. But oh, how few believers carry much of the odor of heaven along with them! How many you might be the means of saving, if you lived a holy, consistent life, if you were evidently a sacrifice bound upon God's altar! Wives might thus, *without the word,* win their husbands, when they see your chaste conversation coupled with fear. Parents might in this way save their children, when they saw you holy and happy. Children have often thus saved their parents. Servants, adorn the doctrine of God your Savior in all things; let your light shine before men. The poorest can do this as well as the richest, the youngest as well as the oldest. Oh, there is no argument like a holy life!

3. *You could seek the salvation of others.* If you have really been brought to Christ and saved, then you know there is a hell, you know that all the unconverted around you are hastening to it; you know there is a Savior, and that He is stretching out His hands all the day long to sinners.

Could you do no more to save sinners than you do? Do you do all you can? You say you *pray for them;* but is it not hypocrisy to pray and do nothing? Will God hear these prayers? Have you no fears that prayers without labors are only provoking God? You say you *cannot speak,* you are not learned. Will that excuse stand in the judgment? Does it require much learning to tell fellow-sinners that they are perishing? If their house was on fire, would it require much learning to wake the sleepers?

Begin at home. Could you not do more for the salvation of those at home? If there are children or servants, have you done all you can for them? Have you done all you can to bring the truth before them, to bring them under a living ministry, to get them to pray and give up sin?

Do you do what you can for your neighbors for years together, and see them on the broad way, without warning them? Do you make a full use of tracts, giving suitable ones to those that need them? Do you persuade Sunday-breakers to go to the house of God? Do you do anything in Sunday schools? Could you not tell little children the way to be saved? Do you do what you can for the *world?* The field is the world.

4. *Feed Christ's poor.* I am far from thinking that

the wicked poor should be passed over, but Christ's poor are our brothers and sisters. Do you do what you can for them? In the great day, Christ will say to those on His right hand, "Come ye blessed, for I was an hungered, and ye gave Me meat." They stand in the place of Christ. Christ does not any more stand in the need of Mary's ointment, or Martha's hospitality, or the Samaritan's drink of water. He is beyond the reach of these things, and will never need them more. But He has left many of His brothers and sisters behind in this world, some diseased, some lame, some like Lazarus all covered with sores; and He says, "What ye do to them, ye do to Me." Do you live plainly, in order to have more to give away? Do you put away vain and gaudy clothes, that you may be able to clothe the naked? Are you thrifty in managing what you have, letting nothing be lost?

Reasons why we should do what we can.

1. *Christ has done what He could for us.* "What could have been done more to My vineyard, that I have not done in it?" (Isa. v. 4). He thought nothing too much to do and to suffer for us. While we were yet sinners, Christ died for us. Greater love than this hath no man. *All his life,* between the manger at Bethlehem and the cross of Calvary, was spent in labors and infinite sufferings for us. All that we needed to suffer, He suffered; all that we need to obey, He obeyed. All His life in glory He spends for us. He ever liveth to make intercession for us. He is head over all things for us; makes everything in all worlds work together for our good. It is all but incredible that each person of the Godhead has made Himself

over to us to be ours. The Father says, "I am thy God;" the Son, "Fear not, for I have redeemed thee;" the Holy Ghost makes us a temple: "I will dwell in them, and walk in them." Is it much that we should do all we can for Him, that we should give ourselves up to Him who gave Himself for us?

2. *Satan does all he can.* Sometimes he comes as a lion; Your adversary the devil, as a roaring lion, walketh about, seeking whom he may devour; sometimes as a serpent, "as the serpent beguiled Eve;" sometimes as an angel of light. He does all he can to tempt and beguile the saints, leading them away by false teachers, injecting blasphemies and polluted thoughts into their minds, casting fiery darts at their souls, stirring up the world to hate and persecute them, stirring up father and mother against the children, and brother against brother. He does all he can to lead captive wicked men, blinding their minds, not allowing them to listen to the Gospel, steeping them in swinish lusts, leading them into despair. When he knows his time is short, he rages all the more. Oh, should not we do all we can, if Satan does all he can?

3. *We have done all we could the other way.* This was one of Paul's great motives for doing all he could: "I thank Christ Jesus our Lord for putting me into the ministry; for I was a blasphemer, and persecutor, and injurious." He never could forget how he had persecuted the Church of God, and wasted it; and this made him as diligent in building it up, and haling men and women to Christ. He preached the faith which once he destroyed.

So with Peter: "Let us live the rest of our time in the flesh not to the lusts of men, but to the will of

God; for the time past of our lives may suffice to have wrought the will of the Gentiles, when we walked in lasciviousness, lusts, excess of wine, revellings, banquetings, and abominable idolatries."

So with John Newton: "How can the old African blasphemer be silent?"

So with many of you. You ran greedily after sin. You were at great pains and cost, and did not spare health, or money, or time, to obtain some sinful gratification. How can you now grudge anything for Christ? Only serve Christ as zealously as you once served the devil.

4. *Christ will own and reward what we do.* The labor that Christ blesseth is believing labor. It is not words of human wisdom, but words of faith, that God makes arrows. The word of a little maid was blessed in the house of Naaman the Syrian. "Follow me" was made the arrow to pierce the heart of Matthew. It is all one to God to save, whether with many, or with them that have no might. If you would do all you can, the town would be filled with the fragrance. Christ will reward it. He defended Mary's work of love, and said it should be spoken of over all the world, and it will yet be told in the judgment. A cup of cold water He will not pass over. "Well done, good and faithful servant."

5. *If you do not do all you can, how can you prove yourself a Christian?* "Pure religion and undefiled before God the Father is this, To visit the fatherless and widows in their affliction, and to keep oneself unspotted from the world." You are greatly mistaken if you think that to be a Christian is merely to have certain views, and convictions, and spiritual delights.

This is all well; but if it leads not to a devoted life, I fear it is all a delusion. If any man be in Christ, he is a new creature.

Let us answer objections.

1. *"The world will mock at us." Answer* This is true. They mocked at Mary. They called it waste and extravagance; and yet, Christ said it was well done. So, if you do what you can, the world will laugh at you, but you will have the smile of Christ. They mocked at Christ when He was full of zeal; they said He was mad and had a devil. They mocked at Paul, and said he was mad; and so with all Christ's living members. "Rejoice, inasmuch as ye are partakers of the sufferings of Christ." "If ye suffer with Him, ye shall also reign with Him."

2. *"What can I do?—I am a woman."* Mary was a woman, yet she did what she could. Mary Magdalene was a woman, and yet she was first at the sepulcher. Phoebe was a woman, yet a support to many, and to Paul also. Dorcas was a woman, yet she made coats and garments for the poor at Joppa. *"I am a child."* Out of the mouth of babes and sucklings God perfects praise. God has often used children in the conversion of their parents.

3. *"I have too little grace to do good."* "He that watereth others, shall be watered himself." "The liberal soul shall be made fat." "It pleased the Father that in Christ should all fullness dwell." There is a full supply of the Spirit to teach you to pray; a full supply of grace to slay your sins and quicken your graces. If you use opportunities of speaking to others, God will give you plenty. If you give much to

God's poor, you shall never want a rich supply. "God is able to make all grace abound toward you; that ye, always having all sufficiency in all things, may abound to every good work." "Bring all the tithes unto my storehouse, and prove me now herewith." "Honor the Lord with thy substance, and with the first-fruits of all thine increase: so shall thy barns be filled with plenty, and thy presses shall burst out with new wine."

April 26, 1842

3

Reasons Why Children Should Fly to Christ Without Delay

"O satisfy us early with thy mercy; that we may rejoice and be glad all our days." —Ps. xc.14.

The late Countess of Huntingdon was not only rich in this world, but rich in faith, and an heir of the kingdom. When she was about nine years of age she saw the dead body of a little child of her own age carried to the grave. She followed the funeral; and it was there that the Holy Spirit first opened her heart to convince her that she needed a Savior. My dear little children, when you look upon the year that has come to an end, may the Holy Spirit bring you to the same conviction. May the still small voice say in your heart, Flee now from the wrath to come. Fly to the Lord Jesus without delay. "Escape for thy life: look not behind thee."

I. *Because life is very short.*

"The days of our years are three-score years and ten; and if by reason of strength they be four-score years, yet is their strength labor and sorrow, for it is soon cut off, and we fly away." Even those who live longest, when they come to die, look back on their life as upon a dream. It is "like a sleep." The hours pass rapidly away during sleep; and when you awake, you hardly know that any time is passed. Such is life. It is like "a tale that is told." When you are listening to an entertaining tale, it fills up the time, and makes the hours steal swiftly by. Even so "we spend our years as a tale that is told."

You have seen a ship upon the river, when the sailors were all on board, the anchor heaved, and the sails spread to the wind, how it glided swiftly past, bounding over the billows. So is it with your days: "They are passed away as the swift ships." Or perhaps you have seen an eagle, when from its nest in the top of the rocks it darts down with quivering wing to seize upon some smaller bird, how swiftly it flies. So is it with your life: it flies "as the eagle hasteth to the prey." You have noticed the mist on the brow of the mountain early in the morning, and you have seen, when the sun rose with his warm, cheering beams, how soon the mist melted away. And "what is your life? It is even a vapor that appeareth for a little time, and then vanisheth away."

Some of you may have seen how short life is in those around you. "Your fathers, where are they? And the prophets, do they live for ever?" How many friends have you lying in the grave! Some of you have more friends in the grave than in this world. They were carried away "as with a flood," and we are fast hastening after them. In a little while the church where you sit will be filled with new worshippers—a new voice will lead the psalm—a new man of God fill the pulpit.

It is an absolute certainty that, in a few years, all

of you who read this will be lying in the grave. Oh, what need, then, to fly to Christ without delay! How great a work you have to do! How short the time you have to do it in! You have to flee from wrath, to come to Christ, to be born again, to receive the Holy Spirit, to be made meet for glory. It is high time that you seek the Lord. The longest lifetime is short enough. Seek conviction of sin and an interest in Christ. "Oh, satisfy me early with Thy mercy, that I may rejoice and be glad all my days."

II. *Because life is very uncertain.*

Men are like grass: "In the morning, it groweth up and flourisheth: in the evening, it is cut down and withereth." Most men are cut down while they are green. More than one-half of the human race die before they reach manhood. In the city of Glasgow alone, more than one-half of the people die before the age of twenty. Of most men it may be said, "He cometh forth as a flower, and is cut down." Death is very certain, but the time is very uncertain.

Some may think they shall not die because they are in good health; but you forget that many die in good health by accidents and other causes. Riches and ease and comforts, good food and good clothing, are no safeguards against dying. It is written, "The rich man also died, and was buried." Kind physicians and kind friends cannot keep you from dying. When death comes, he laughs at the efforts of physicians— he tears you from the tenderest arms.

Some think they shall not die because they are not prepared to die. But you forget that most people die unprepared, unconverted, unsaved. You forget that it is written of the strait gate, "Few there be that find it." Most people lie down in a dark grave, and a darker eternity.

Some of you may think you shall not die because you are young. You forget that one-half of the human race die before they reach manhood. The half of the inhabitants of this place die before they are twenty. Oh, if you had to stand as often as I have beside the dying bed of little children—to see their wild looks and outstretched hands, and to hear their dying cries—you would see how needful it is to fly to Christ now.

It may be your turn next. Are you prepared to die? Have you fled for refuge to Jesus? Have you found forgiveness? "Boast not thyself of tomorrow; for thou knowest not what a day may bring forth."

III. *Most that are ever saved fly to Christ when young.*

It was so in the days of our blessed Savior. Those that were come to years were too wise and prudent to be saved by the blood of the Son of God, and He revealed it to those that were younger and had less wisdom. "I thank Thee, O Father, Lord of heaven and earth, because Thou hast hidden these things from the wise and prudent, and revealed them unto babes. Even so, Father, for so it seemed good in Thy sight." "He gathers the lambs with His arm, and carries them in His bosom." So it has been in almost all times of the revival of religion. If you ask aged Christians, most of them will tell you that they were made anxious about their souls when young.

Oh, what a reason is here for seeking an early inbringing to Christ! If you are not saved in youth, it is likely you never will. There is a tide in the affairs of souls. There are times which may be called converting times. All holy times are peculiarly converting times. Sunday is the great day for gathering in souls—it is Christ's market-day. It is the great harvest-day of souls. I know there is a generation rising up that would fain trample Sunday beneath their feet: but prize you the day of rest.

The time of affliction is converting time. When God takes away those you love best, and you say, "This is the finger of God," remember it is Christ wanting to get in to save you: open the door and let Him in. The time of the striving of the Holy Spirit is converting time. If you feel your heart pricked in reading the Bible, or in hearing your teacher, "quench not the Spirit;" "resist not the Holy Ghost;" "grieve not the Holy Spirit of God."

Youth is converting time. "Suffer little children to come unto Me, and forbid them not." Oh, you that are lambs, seek to be gathered with the arm of the Savior, and carried in His gentle bosom. Come to trust under the Savior's wings. "Yet there is room."

IV. *Because it is happier to be in Christ than out of Christ.*

Many that read these words are saying in their heart, It is a dull thing to be religious. Youth is the time for pleasure—the time to eat, drink, and be merry; to rise up to play. Now, I know that youth is the time for pleasure; the foot is more elastic then, the eye more full of life, the heart more full of gladness. But that is the very reason why I say youth is the time to fly to Christ. It is far happier to be in

Christ than to be out of Christ.

It satisfies the heart. I never will deny that there are pleasures to be found out of Christ. The song and the dance, and the exciting game, are most engaging to young hearts. But ah! think a moment. Is it not an awful thing to be happy when you are unsaved? Would it not be dreadful to see a man sleeping in a house all on fire? And is it not enough to make one shudder to see you dancing and making merry when God is angry with you every day?

Think again. Are there not infinitely sweeter pleasures to be had in Christ? "Whoso drinketh of this water shall thirst again; but whoso drinketh of the water that I shall give him shall never thirst." "In Thy presence is fullness of joy: at Thy right hand are pleasures for evermore." To be forgiven, to be at peace with God, to have Him for a father, to have Him loving us and smiling on us, to have the Holy Spirit coming into our hearts, and making us holy, this is worth a whole eternity of your pleasures. "A day in Thy courts is better than a thousand." Oh to be "satisfied with favor, and full with the blessing of the Lord!" Your daily bread becomes sweeter. You eat your meat "with gladness and singleness of heart, praising God." Your foot is more light and bounding, for it bears a ransomed body. Your sleep is sweeter at night, for "so He giveth His beloved sleep." The sun shines more lovingly, and the earth wears a pleasanter smile, because you can say, "My Father made them all."

It makes you glad all your days. The pleasures of sin are only "for a season;" they do not last. But to be brought to Christ is like the dawning of an eternal day; it spreads the serenity of heaven over all the days of our pilgrimage. In suffering days, what will the world do for you?

"Like vinegar upon niter, so is he that singeth songs to a heavy heart." Believe me there are days at hand when you will "say of laughter, It is mad; and of mirth, What doth it?" But if you fly to Jesus Christ now, He will cheer you in the days of darkness. When the winds are contrary and the waves are high, Jesus will draw near, and say, "Be not afraid; it is I." That voice stills the heart in the stormiest hour. When the world reproaches you and casts out your name as evil—when the doors are shut—Jesus will come in, and say, "Peace be unto you." Who can tell the sweetness and the peace which Jesus gives in such an hour?

One little girl that was early brought to Christ felt this when long confined to a sick-bed. "I am not weary of my bed," she said, "for my bed is green, and all that I meet with is perfumed with love to me. The time, night and day, is made sweet to me by the Lord. When it is evening, it is pleasant; and when it is morning, I am refreshed."

Last of all, in a dying day, what will the world do for you? The dance and the song, and the merry companion, will then lose all their power to cheer you. Not one jest more; not one smile more. "Oh that you were wise, that you would understand this, and consider your latter end!" But that is the very time when the soul of one in Christ rejoices with a joy unspeakable and full of glory.

"Jesus can make a dying bed softer than downy pillows are." You remember, when Stephen came to die, his gentle breast battered with cruel stones; but he kneeled down and said, "Lord Jesus, receive my spirit." John Newton tells us a Christian girl who, on her dying day, said, "If this be dying, it is a pleasant thing to die." Another little Christian, of eight years of age, came home ill of the malady of which he died. His mother asked him if he were afraid to die. "No," said he, "I wish to die, if it be God's will: that sweet word, 'Sleep in Jesus,' makes me happy when I think on the grave."

"My little children, of whom I travail in birth again till Christ be formed in you," if you would live happy and die happy, come now to the Savior. The door of the ark is wide open. Enter now or it may be never.

Children Called To Christ

Like mist on the mountain,
　Like ships on the sea,
So swiftly the years
　Of our pilgrimage flee;
In the grave of our fathers
　How soon shall we lie!
Dear children, today
　To a Savior fly.

How sweet are the flowerets
　In April and May!
But often the frost makes
　Them wither away.
Like flowers you may fade:
　Are you ready to die?
While "yet there is room,"
　To a Savior fly.

When Samuel was young,
　　He first knew the Lord,
He slept in His smile
　　And rejoiced in His word:
So most of God's children
　　Are early brought nigh:
Oh, seek Him in youth—
　　To a Savior fly.

Do you ask me for pleasure?
　　Then lean on His breast,
From there the sin-laden
　　And weary find rest.
In the valley of death
　　You will triumphing cry—
"If this be called dying,
　　'Tis pleasant to die!"

The Child Coming To Jesus

Suffer me to come to Jesus,
　　Mother, dear, forbid me not;
By His blood from hell He frees us,
　　Makes us fair without a spot.

Suffer me, my earthly father,
　　At His pierced feet to fall:
Why forbid me? help me, rather;
　　Jesus is my all in all.

Suffer me to run unto Him:
　　Gentle sisters, come with me.
Oh, that all I love but knew Him!
　　Then my home a heaven would be.

Loving playmates, gay and smiling,
　　Bid me not forsake the cross;

Hard to bear is your reviling,
 Yet for Jesus all is dross.

Yes, though all the world have chide me,
 Father, mother, sister, friend—
Jesus never will forbid me!
 Jesus loves me to the end!

Gentle shepherd, on Thy shoulder
 Carry me, a sinful lamb;
Give me faith, and make me bolder,
 Till with Thee in heaven I am.

4

Miscellaneous Quotes
(arranged by topic)

Evangelism

I have often told you that a work of revival in any place almost always begins with the children of God. God pours water first on "him that is thirsty," and then on the dry ground. But how little has "the word of the Lord sounded out from you"! I do not mean that you should have been loud talkers about religious things. But you should have been "living epistles, known and read of all men." If you had day by day the blood of Christ upon your conscience, how many of your friends and neighbors that are going down to hell might have been saying this day, "Thy people shall be my people, and thy God my God"! Think, my beloved friends, that every act of unholiness, of conformity to the world, of selfishness, of whispering and backbiting, is hindering the work of God in the parish, and ruining souls eternally.

As I was walking through the fields, the thought came over me with almost overwhelming power, that every one of my flock must soon be in heaven or hell. Oh, how I wished that I had a tongue like thunder, that I might make all hear. Or that I had a frame like iron, that I might visit every one, and say, "Escape for thy life!" Ah, sinners! you little know how I fear that you will lay the blame of your damnation at my door.

Suffering

I hope this affliction will be blessed to me. I always feel much need of God's afflicting hand. In the whirl of active labor there is so little time for watching and for bewailing, and seeking grace to oppose the sins of our ministry, that I always feel it a blessed thing when the Savior takes me aside from the crowd, as he took the blind man out of the town, and removes the veil, and clears away obscuring mists, and by His word and Spirit leads to deeper peace and a holier walk. Ah! There is nothing like a calm look into the eternal world to teach us the emptiness of human praise, the sinfulness of self-seeking and vain glory, to teach us the preciousness of Christ, who is called "the tried stone."

You cannot love trouble for its own sake; bitter must always be bitter, and pain must always be pain. God knows you cannot love trouble. Yet for the blessings that it brings, He can make you pray for it. Does trouble work patience in you? Does it lead you to cling closer to the Lord Jesus—to hide deeper in the rock? Does it make you "be still and know that He is God"? Does it make you lie passive in His hand, and know no will but His?

Thus does patience work experience—an experimental acquaintance with Jesus. Does it bring you a fuller taste of His sweetness, so that you know whom you have believed? And does this experience give you further hope of glory—another anchor cast within the veil? And does this hope give you a heart that cannot be ashamed, because you are convinced that God has loved you, and will love you to the end? Ah! then you have got the improvement through trouble, if it has led you thus.

Life in Christ

Observe it is said, "trust in the Lord with all thine heart." When you believe in Jesus for righteousness, you must cast away all your own claims for pardon. Your own righteousness must be filthy rags in your eyes. You must come empty, that you may go away full of Jesus. And just so, when you trust in Jesus for strength, you must cast away all your natural notions of your own strength; you must feel that your own resolutions, and vows, and promises, are as useless to stem the current of your passions, as so many straws would be in stemming the mightiest waterfall. You must feel that your own firmness and manliness of disposition, which has so long been the praise of your friends and the boast of your own mind, are as powerless, before the breath of temptation, as a broken reed before the hurricane. You must feel that you wrestle not with flesh and blood, but with spirits of gigantic power, in whose mighty grasp you are feeble as a child. Then, and then only will you come with all your heart to trust in the Lord your strength. When the believer is weakest, then he is the strongest.

When you came to us weary and heavy laden with guilt, we pointed you to Jesus, for He is the Lord our righteousness. When you come to us again, groaning under the power of indwelling sin, we point you again to Jesus, for He is the Lord our strength. It is the true mark of a false and ignorant physician of bodies, when to every sufferer, whatever be the disease, he applies the same remedy. But it is the true mark of a good and faithful physician of souls, when, to every sick and perishing soul, in every stage of the disease, he brings the one, the only remedy, the only balm in Gilead.

Christ was anointed not only to bind up the broken-hearted, but also to proclaim liberty to the captives. If it be good and wise to direct the poor broken-hearted sinner, who has no way of justifying himself, to Jesus, as his righteousness, it must be just as good and wise to direct the poor believer, groaning under the bondage of corruption, having no way to sanctify himself, to look to Jesus as his wisdom, his sanctification, his redemption. Thou hast once looked unto Jesus as thy covenant head, bearing all wrath, fulfilling all righteousness in thy stead, and that gave thee peace. Well, look again to the same Jesus as thy covenant head, obtaining by his merits gifts for men, even the promise of the Father, to shed down on all his members; and let that also give thee peace.

"Trust in the Lord with all thine heart." Thou hast looked to Jesus on the cross, and that gave thee peace of conscience. Look to Him now upon the throne, and that will give thee purity of heart. I know of but one way in which a branch can be made a leafy, healthy, fruit-bearing branch; and that is by being grafted into the vine and abiding there. And just so I know of but one way in which a believer can be made a holy, happy and fruitful child of God; and that is by believing in Jesus, abiding in Him, walking in Him, being rooted and built up in Him.

Whoever, then, would live a life of persevering holiness, let him keep his eye fixed on the Savior. As long as Peter looked only to the Savior, he walked upon the sea in safety, to go to Jesus. But when he looked around and saw the wind boisterous, he was afraid, and beginning to sink, cried, "Lord, save me!" Just so will it be with you. As long as you look believingly to the Savior, who loved you, and gave Himself for you, so long you may tread the waters of life's troubled sea, and the soles of your feet shall not be wet. But venture to look around upon the winds and waves that threaten you on every hand, and, like Peter, you begin to sink, and cry, "Lord, save me!" How justly, then, may we address to you the Savior's rebuke to Peter; "O thou of little faith, wherefore didst thou doubt?" Look again to the love of the Savior, and behold that love which constrains you to live no more to yourself, but to Him that died for you and rose again.

Look to Christ; for the glorious Son of God so loved lost souls, that He took on Him a body and died for us—bore our curse, and obeyed the law in our place. Look to Him and live. You need no preparation, you need no endeavors, you need no duties, you need no strivings, you only need to look and live.

Seek to be made holier every day; pray, strive, wrestle for the Spirit, to make you like God. Be as much as you can with God. I declare to you that I had rather be one hour with God, than a thousand with the sweetest society on earth or in heaven. All other joys are but streams; God is the fountain: "all my springs are in Thee." Now may the blessings that are on the head of the just be on your head. Be faithful unto death, and Christ will give you a crown of life.

I trust you feel real desire after complete holiness. This is the truest mark of being born again. It is a mark that He has made us meet for the inheritance of the saints in light. If a nobleman were to adopt a beggar boy, he would not only feed and clothe him, but educate him, and fit him to move in the sphere into which he was afterwards to be brought; and if you saw this boy filled with a noble spirit, you would say he is meet to be put among the children. So may you be made meet for glory. The farmer does not cut down his wheat till it is ripe. So does the Lord Jesus: He first ripens the soul, then gathers it into His barn.

I want my life to be hid with Christ in God. At present there is too much hurry and bustle, and outward working, to allow the calm working of the Spirit on the heart. I seldom get time to meditate, like Isaac, at eveningtide, except when I am tired. But the dew comes down when all nature is at rest, when every leaf is still.

Speak for eternity. Above all things, cultivate your own spirit. A word spoken by you when your conscience is clear and your heart full of God's Spirit, is worth ten thousand words spoken in unbelief and sin. Remember it is God, and not man, that must have the glory. It is not much speaking, but much faith, that is needed.

Seek advance of personal holiness. It is for this that the grace of God has appeared to you. For this Jesus died; for this He chose you; for this He converted you—to make you holy men, living epistles of Christ, monuments of what God can do in a sinner's heart. You know what true holiness is. It is Christ in you the hope of glory. Let Him dwell in you, and so all His features will shine in your hearts and faces. Oh, to be like Jesus! This is heaven, wherever it be.

Bible/Prayer

You read your Bible regularly, of course; but do try and understand it, and still more, to feel it. Read more parts than one at a time. For example, if you are reading Genesis, read a Psalm also. If you are reading Matthew, read a small bit of an epistle also.

Turn the Bible into prayer. Thus, if you are reading the first Psalm, spread the Bible on the chair before you, kneel and pray, "Let me not stand in the counsel of the ungodly." This is the best way of knowing the meaning of the Bible, and of learning to pray. In prayer confess your sins by name, going over those of the past day one by one.

Pray for your friends by name. If you love them, surely you will pray for their souls. I know well that there are prayers constantly ascending for you from your own house; and will you not pray for them back again? Do this regularly. If you pray sincerely for others, it will make you pray for yourself.

You have hindered God's work by your want of prayer. When God gives grace to souls, it is in answer to the prayers of His children. You will see this on the day of Pentecost. Ezek. 37:9 shows that in answer to the prayer of a single child of God, God will give grace to a whole valley full of dry and prayerless bones. Where God puts it into the heart of His children to pray, it is certain that He is going to pour down His Spirit in abundance.

"Now, where have been your prayers, O children of God?" The salvation of those around you depends on your asking. Dear Christians, I often think it strange that ever we should be in heaven, and so many in hell through our soul-destroying carelessness. The good Lord pardon the past, and stir you up for the future. Plead and wrestle with God, showing Him that the cause is His own, and that it is all for His own glory to arise and have mercy upon Zion.

5

Daily Bible Calendar

Jesus prayed "Sanctify them through Thy truth. Thy word is truth" (John 17:17).

The Apostle Paul wrote, "All Scripture is given by inspiration of God, and is profitable for doctrine, for reproof, for correction, for instruction in righteousness; that the man of God may be perfect, thoroughly furnished unto all good works" (2 Timothy 3:16–17).

Robert Murray McCheyne said that if you follow this calendar, the entire Bible will be read through completely in the course of a year—the Old Testament once, the New Testament and Psalms twice. He wrote, "I fear many of you never read the whole Bible; and yet it is all equally divine. If we pass over some parts of Scripture, we shall be incomplete Christians."

Part of this introduction and the following calendar were arranged by Robert Murray McCheyne in 1844.

JANUARY *"This is my beloved Son, in whom I am well pleased: hear ye Him."*

Day	Family Reading	Secret Reading
1	Genesis 1 Matthew 1	Ezra 1 Acts 1
2	Genesis 2 Matthew 2	Ezra 2 Acts 2
3	Genesis 3 Matthew 3	Ezra 3 Acts 3
4	Genesis 4 Matthew 4	Ezra 4 Acts 4
5	Genesis 5 Matthew 5	Ezra 5 Acts 5
6	Genesis 6 Matthew 6	Ezra 6 Acts 6
7	Genesis 7 Matthew 7	Ezra 7 Acts 7
8	Genesis 8 Matthew 8	Ezra 8 Acts 8
9	Genesis 9, 10 Matthew 9	Ezra 9 Acts 9
10	Genesis 11 Matthew 10	Ezra 10 Acts 10
11	Genesis 12 Matthew 11	Nehemiah 1 Acts 11
12	Genesis 13 Matthew 12	Nehemiah 2 Acts 12
13	Genesis 14 Matthew 13	Nehemiah 3 Acts 13
14	Genesis 15 Matthew 14	Nehemiah 4 Acts 14

15	Genesis 16 Matthew 15	Nehemiah 5 Acts 15
16	Genesis 17 Matthew 16	Nehemiah 6 Acts 16
17	Genesis 18 Matthew 17	Nehemiah 7 Acts 17
18	Genesis 19 Matthew 18	Nehemiah 8 Acts 18
19	Genesis 20 Matthew 19	Nehemiah 9 Acts 19
20	Genesis 21 Matthew 20	Nehemiah 10 Acts 20
21	Genesis 22 Matthew 21	Nehemiah 11 Acts 21
22	Genesis 23 Matthew 22	Nehemiah 12 Acts 22
23	Genesis 24 Matthew 23	Nehemiah 13 Acts 23
24	Genesis 25 Matthew 24	Esther 1 Acts 24
25	Genesis 26 Matthew 25	Esther 2 Acts 25
26	Genesis 27 Matthew 26	Esther 3 Acts 26
27	Genesis 28 Matthew 27	Esther 4 Acts 27
28	Genesis 29 Matthew 28	Esther 5 Acts 28
29	Genesis 30 Mark 1	Esther 6 Romans 1
30	Genesis 31 Mark 2	Esther 7 Romans 2

| 31 | Genesis 32 | Esther 8 |
| | Mark 3 | Romans 3 |

FEBRUARY *"I have esteemed the words of His mouth more than my necessary food."*

Day	**Family Reading**	**Secret Reading**
1	Genesis 33	Esther 9, 10
	Mark 4	Romans 4
2	Genesis 34	Job 1
	Mark 5	Romans 5
3	Genesis 35, 36	Job 2
	Mark 6	Romans 6
4	Genesis 37	Job 3
	Mark 7	Romans 7
5	Genesis 38	Job 4
	Mark 8	Romans 8
6	Genesis 39	Job 5
	Mark 9	Romans 9
7	Genesis 40	Job 6
	Mark 10	Romans 10
8	Genesis 41	Job 7
	Mark 11	Romans 11
9	Genesis 42	Job 8
	Mark 12	Romans 12
10	Genesis 43	Job 9
	Mark 13	Romans 13
11	Genesis 44	Job 10
	Mark 14	Romans 14
12	Genesis 45	Job 11
	Mark 15	Romans 15
13	Genesis 46	Job 12
	Mark 16	Romans 16

14	Genesis 47 Luke 1:1–38	Job 13 1 Corinthians 1
15	Genesis 48 Luke 1:39–80	Job 14 1 Corinthians 2
16	Genesis 49 Luke 2	Job 15 1 Corinthians 3
17	Genesis 50 Luke 3	Job 16, 17 1 Corinthians 4
18	Exodus 1 Luke 4	Job 18 1 Corinthians 5
19	Exodus 2 Luke 5	Job 19 1 Corinthians 6
20	Exodus 3 Luke 6	Job 20 1 Corinthians 7
21	Exodus 4 Luke 7	Job 21 1 Corinthians 8
22	Exodus 5 Luke 8	Job 22 1 Corinthians 9
23	Exodus 6 Luke 9	Job 23 1 Corinthians 10
24	Exodus 7 Luke 10	Job 24 1 Corinthians 11
25	Exodus 8 Luke 11	Job 25, 26 1 Corinthians 12
26	Exodus 9 Luke 12	Job 27 1 Corinthians 13
27	Exodus 10 Luke 13	Job 28 1 Corinthians 14
28	Exodus 11, 12:1–21 Luke 14	Job 29 1 Corinthians 15

MARCH *"Mary kept all these things, and pondered them in her heart."*

Day	Family Reading	Secret Reading
1	Exodus 12:22–51 Luke 15	Job 30 1 Corinthians 16
2	Exodus 13 Luke 16	Job 31 2 Corinthians 1
3	Exodus 14 Luke 17	Job 32 2 Corinthians 2
4	Exodus 15 Luke 18	Job 33 2 Corinthians 3
5	Exodus 16 Luke 19	Job 34 2 Corinthians 4
6	Exodus 17 Luke 20	Job 35 2 Corinthians 5
7	Exodus 18 Luke 21	Job 36 2 Corinthians 6
8	Exodus 19 Luke 22	Job 37 2 Corinthians 7
9	Exodus 20 Luke 23	Job 38 2 Corinthians 8
10	Exodus 21 Luke 24	Job 39 2 Corinthians 9
11	Exodus 22 John 1	Job 40 2 Corinthians 10
12	Exodus 23 John 2	Job 41 2 Corinthians 11
13	Exodus 24 John 3	Job 42 2 Corinthians 12
14	Exodus 25 John 4	Proverbs 1 2 Corinthians 13

15	Exodus 26 John 5	Proverbs 2 Galatians 1
16	Exodus 27 John 6	Proverbs 3 Galatians 2
17	Exodus 28 John 7	Proverbs 4 Galatians 3
18	Exodus 29 John 8	Proverbs 5 Galatians 4
19	Exodus 30 John 9	Proverbs 6 Galatians 5
20	Exodus 31 John 10	Proverbs 7 Galatians 6
21	Exodus 32 John 11	Proverbs 8 Ephesians 1
22	Exodus 33 John 12	Proverbs 9 Ephesians 2
23	Exodus 34 John 13	Proverbs 10 Ephesians 3
24	Exodus 35 John 14	Proverbs 11 Ephesians 4
25	Exodus 36 John 15	Proverbs 12 Ephesians 5
26	Exodus 37 John 16	Proverbs 13 Ephesians 6
27	Exodus 38 John 17	Proverbs 14 Philippians 1
28	Exodus 39 John 18	Proverbs 15 Philippians 2
29	Exodus 40 John 19	Proverbs 16 Philippians 3
30	Leviticus 1 John 20	Proverbs 17 Philippians 4

| 31 | Leviticus 2, 3 | Proverbs 18 |
| | John 21 | Colossians 1 |

APRIL *"O send out Thy light and Thy truth; let them lead me."*

Day	Family Reading	Secret Reading
1	Leviticus 4 Psalms 1, 2	Proverbs 19 Colossians 2
2	Leviticus 5 Psalms 3, 4	Proverbs 20 Colossians 3
3	Leviticus 6 Psalms 5, 6	Proverbs 21 Colossians 4
4	Leviticus 7 Psalms 7, 8	Proverbs 22 1 Thessalonians 1
5	Leviticus 8 Psalms 9	Proverbs 23 1 Thessalonians 2
6	Leviticus 9 Psalms 10	Proverbs 24 1 Thessalonians 3
7	Leviticus 10 Psalms 11, 12	Proverbs 25 1 Thessalonians 4
8	Leviticus 11, 12 Psalms 13, 14	Proverbs 26 1 Thessalonians 5
9	Leviticus 13 Psalms 15, 16	Proverbs 27 2 Thessalonians 1
10	Leviticus 14 Psalms 17	Proverbs 28 2 Thessalonians 2
11	Leviticus 15 Psalms 18	Proverbs 29 2 Thessalonians 3
12	Leviticus 16 Psalms 19	Proverbs 30 1 Timothy 1
13	Leviticus 17 Psalms 20, 21	Proverbs 31 1 Timothy 2

14	Leviticus 18 Psalms 22	Ecclesiastes 1 1 Timothy 3
15	Leviticus 19 Psalms 23, 24	Ecclesiastes 2 1 Timothy 4
16	Leviticus 20 Psalms 25	Ecclesiastes 3 1 Timothy 5
17	Leviticus 21 Psalms 26, 27	Ecclesiastes 4 1 Timothy 6
18	Leviticus 22 Psalms 28, 29	Ecclesiastes 5 2 Timothy 1
19	Leviticus 23 Psalms 30	Ecclesiastes 6 2 Timothy 2
20	Leviticus 24 Psalms 31	Ecclesiastes 7 2 Timothy 3
21	Leviticus 25 Psalms 32	Ecclesiastes 8 2 Timothy 4
22	Leviticus 26 Psalms 33	Ecclesiastes 9 Titus 1
23	Leviticus 27 Psalms 34	Ecclesiastes 10 Titus 2
24	Numbers 1 Psalms 35	Ecclesiastes 11 Titus 3
25	Numbers 2 Psalms 36	Ecclesiastes 12 Philemon 1
26	Numbers 3 Psalms 37	Song of S. 1 Hebrews 1
27	Numbers 4 Psalms 38	Song of S. 2 Hebrews 2
28	Numbers 5 Psalms 39	Song of S. 3 Hebrews 3
29	Numbers 6 Psalms 40, 41	Song of S. 4 Hebrews 4

| 30 | Numbers 7 | Song of S. 5 |
| | Psalms 42, 43 | Hebrews 5 |

MAY *"From a child thou hast known thy holy Scriptures."*

Day	**Family Reading**	**Secret Reading**
1	Numbers 8 Psalms 44	Song of S. 6 Hebrews 6
2	Numbers 9 Psalms 45	Song of S. 7 Hebrews 7
3	Numbers 10 Psalms 46, 47	Song of S. 8 Hebrews 8
4	Numbers 11 Psalms 48	Isaiah 1 Hebrews 9
5	Numbers 12, 13 Psalms 49	Isaiah 2 Hebrews 10
6	Numbers 14 Psalms 50	Isaiah 3, 4 Hebrews 11
7	Numbers 15 Psalms 51	Isaiah 5 Hebrews 12
8	Numbers 16 Psalms 52–54	Isaiah 6 Hebrews 13
9	Numbers 17, 18 Psalms 55	Isaiah 7 James 1
10	Numbers 19 Psalms 56, 57	Isaiah 8, 9:1–7 James 2
11	Numbers 20 Psalms 58, 59	Isaiah 9:8–10:4 James 3
12	Numbers 21 Psalms 60, 61	Isaiah 10:5–34 James 4
13	Numbers 22 Psalms 62, 63	Isaiah 11, 12 James 5

14	Numbers 23 Psalms 64, 65	Isaiah 13 1 Peter 1
15	Numbers 24 Psalms 66, 67	Isaiah 14 1 Peter 2
16	Numbers 25 Psalms 68	Isaiah 15 1 Peter 3
17	Numbers 26 Psalms 69	Isaiah 16 1 Peter 4
18	Numbers 27 Psalms 70, 71	Isaiah 17, 18 1 Peter 5
19	Numbers 28 Psalms 72	Isaiah 19, 20 2 Peter 1
20	Numbers 29 Psalms 73	Isaiah 21 2 Peter 2
21	Numbers 30 Psalms 74	Isaiah 22 2 Peter 3
22	Numbers 31 Psalms 75, 76	Isaiah 23 1 John 1
23	Numbers 32 Psalms 77	Isaiah 24 1 John 2
24	Numbers 33 Psalms 78:1–37	Isaiah 25 1 John 3
25	Numbers 34 Psalms 78:38–72	Isaiah 26 1 John 4
26	Numbers 35 Psalms 79	Isaiah 27 1 John 5
27	Numbers 36 Psalms 80	Isaiah 28 2 John 1
28	Deuteronomy 1 Psalms 81, 82	Isaiah 29 3 John 1
29	Deuteronomy 2 Psalms 83, 84	Isaiah 30 Jude 1

| 30 | Deuteronomy 3
Psalms 85 | Isaiah 31
Revelation 1 |
| 31 | Deuteronomy 4
Psalms 86, 87 | Isaiah 32
Revelation 2 |

JUNE *"Blessed is he that readeth and they that hear."*

Day	Family Reading	Secret Reading
1	Deuteronomy 5 Psalms 88	Isaiah 33 Revelation 3
2	Deuteronomy 6 Psalms 89	Isaiah 34 Revelation 4
3	Deuteronomy 7 Psalms 90	Isaiah 35 Revelation 5
4	Deuteronomy 8 Psalms 91	Isaiah 36 Revelation 6
5	Deuteronomy 9 Psalms 92, 93	Isaiah 37 Revelation 7
6	Deuteronomy 10 Psalms 94	Isaiah 38 Revelation 8
7	Deuteronomy 11 Psalms 95, 96	Isaiah 39 Revelation 9
8	Deuteronomy 12 Psalms 97, 98	Isaiah 40 Revelation 10
9	Deuteronomy 13, 14 Psalms 99–101	Isaiah 41 Revelation 11
10	Deuteronomy 15 Psalms 102	Isaiah 42 Revelation 12
11	Deuteronomy 16 Psalms 103	Isaiah 43 Revelation 13
12	Deuteronomy 17 Psalms 104	Isaiah 44 Revelation 14

13	Deuteronomy 18 Psalms 105	Isaiah 45 Revelation 15
14	Deuteronomy 19 Psalms 106	Isaiah 46 Revelation 16
15	Deuteronomy 20 Psalms 107	Isaiah 47 Revelation 17
16	Deuteronomy 21 Psalms 108, 109	Isaiah 48 Revelation 18
17	Deuteronomy 22 Psalms 110, 111	Isaiah 49 Revelation 19
18	Deuteronomy 23 Psalms 112, 113	Isaiah 50 Revelation 20
19	Deuteronomy 24 Psalms 114, 115	Isaiah 51 Revelation 21
20	Deuteronomy 25 Psalms 116	Isaiah 52 Revelation 22
21	Deuteronomy 26 Psalms 117, 118	Isaiah 53 Matthew 1
22	Deuteronomy 27, 28:1–19 Psalms 119:1–24	Isaiah 54 Matthew 2
23	Deuteronomy 28:20–68 Psalms 119:25–48	Isaiah 55 Matthew 3
24	Deuteronomy 29 Psalms 119:49–72	Isaiah 56 Matthew 4
25	Deuteronomy 30 Psalms 119:73–96	Isaiah 57 Matthew 5
26	Deuteronomy 31 Psalms 119:97–120	Isaiah 58 Matthew 6
27	Deuteronomy 32 Psalms 119:121–144	Isaiah 59 Matthew 7

28	Deuteronomy 33, 34	Isaiah 60
	Psalms 119:145–176	Matthew 8
29	Joshua 1	Isaiah 61
	Psalms 120–122	Matthew 9
30	Joshua 2	Isaiah 62
	Psalms 123–125	Matthew 10

JULY *"They received the word with all readiness of mind, and searched the Scriptures daily."*

Day	Family Reading	Secret Reading
1	Joshua 3	Isaiah 63
	Psalms 126–128	Matthew 11
2	Joshua 4	Isaiah 64
	Psalms 129–131	Matthew 12
3	Joshua 5, 6:1–5	Isaiah 65
	Psalms 132–134	Matthew 13
4	Joshua 6:6–27	Isaiah 66
	Psalms 135, 136	Matthew 14
5	Joshua 7	Jeremiah 1
	Psalms 137, 138	Matthew 15
6	Joshua 8	Jeremiah 2
	Psalms 139	Matthew 16
7	Joshua 9	Jeremiah 3
	Psalms 140, 141	Matthew 17

8	Joshua 10 Psalms 142, 143	Jeremiah 4 Matthew 18
9	Joshua 11 Psalms 144	Jeremiah 5 Matthew 19
10	Joshua 12, 13 Psalms 145	Jeremiah 6 Matthew 20
11	Joshua 14, 15 Psalms 146, 147	Jeremiah 7 Matthew 21
12	Joshua 16, 17 Psalms 148	Jeremiah 8 Matthew 22
13	Joshua 18, 19 Psalms 149, 150	Jeremiah 9 Matthew 23
14	Joshua 20, 21 Acts 1	Jeremiah 10 Matthew 24
15	Joshua 22 Acts 2	Jeremiah 11 Matthew 25
16	Joshua 23 Acts 3	Jeremiah 12 Matthew 26
17	Joshua 24 Acts 4	Jeremiah 13 Matthew 27
18	Judges 1 Acts 5	Jeremiah 14 Matthew 28
19	Judges 2 Acts 6	Jeremiah 15 Mark 1
20	Judges 3 Acts 7	Jeremiah 16 Mark 2
21	Judges 4 Acts 8	Jeremiah 17 Mark 3
22	Judges 5 Acts 9	Jeremiah 18 Mark 4
23	Judges 6 Acts 10	Jeremiah 19 Mark 5

24	Judges 7 Acts 11	Jeremiah 20 Mark 6
25	Judges 8 Acts 12	Jeremiah 21 Mark 7
26	Judges 9 Acts 13	Jeremiah 22 Mark 8
27	Judges 10, 11:1–11 Acts 14	Jeremiah 23 Mark 9
28	Judges 11:12–40 Acts 15	Jeremiah 24 Mark 10
29	Judges 12 Acts 16	Jeremiah 25 Mark 11
30	Judges 13 Acts 17	Jeremiah 26 Mark 12
31	Judges 14 Acts 18	Jeremiah 27 Mark 13

AUGUST	*"Speak, Lord; for Thy servant heareth."*	
Day	**Family Reading**	**Secret Reading**
1	Judges 15 Acts 19	Jeremiah 28 Mark 14
2	Judges 16 Acts 20	Jeremiah 29 Mark 15
3	Judges 17 Acts 21	Jeremiah 30, 31 Mark 16
4	Judges 18 Acts 22	Jeremiah 32 Psalms 1, 2
5	Judges 19 Acts 23	Jeremiah 33 Psalms 3, 4
6	Judges 20 Acts 24	Jeremiah 34 Psalms 5, 6

7	Judges 21 Acts 25	Jeremiah 35 Psalms 7, 8
8	Ruth 1 Acts 26	Jeremiah 36, 45 Psalms 9
9	Ruth 2 Acts 27	Jeremiah 37 Psalms 10
10	Ruth 3, 4 Acts 28	Jeremiah 38 Psalms 11, 12
11	1 Samuel 1 Romans 1	Jeremiah 39 Psalms 13, 14
12	1 Samuel 2 Romans 2	Jeremiah 40 Psalms 15, 16
13	1 Samuel 3 Romans 3	Jeremiah 41 Psalms 17
14	1 Samuel 4 Romans 4	Jeremiah 42 Psalms 18
15	1 Samuel 5, 6 Romans 5	Jeremiah 43 Psalms 19
16	1 Samuel 7, 8 Romans 6	Jeremiah 44 Psalms 20, 21
17	1 Samuel 9 Romans 7	Jeremiah 46 Psalms 22
18	1 Samuel 10 Romans 8	Jeremiah 47 Psalms 23, 24
19	1 Samuel 11 Romans 9	Jeremiah 48 Psalms 25
20	1 Samuel 12 Romans 10	Jeremiah 49 Psalms 26, 27
21	1 Samuel 13 Romans 11	Jeremiah 50 Psalms 28, 29
22	1 Samuel 14 Romans 12	Jeremiah 51 Psalms 30

23	1 Samuel 15 Romans 13	Jeremiah 52 Psalms 31
24	1 Samuel 16 Romans 14	Lamentations 1 Psalms 32
25	1 Samuel 17 Romans 15	Lamentations 2 Psalms 33
26	1 Samuel 18 Romans 16	Lamentations 3 Psalms 34
27	1 Samuel 19 1 Corinthians 1	Lamentations 4 Psalms 35
28	1 Samuel 20 1 Corinthians 2	Lamentations 5 Psalms 36
29	1 Samuel 21, 22 1 Corinthians 3	Ezekiel 1 Psalms 37
30	1 Samuel 23 1 Corinthians 4	Ezekiel 2 Psalms 38
31	1 Samuel 24 1 Corinthians 5	Ezekiel 3 Psalms 39

SEPTEMBER *"The law of the Lord is perfect, converting the soul."*

Day	Family Reading	Secret Reading
1	1 Samuel 25 1 Corinthians 6	Ezekiel 4 Psalms 40, 41
2	1 Samuel 26 1 Corinthians 7	Ezekiel 5 Psalms 42, 43
3	1 Samuel 27 1 Corinthians 8	Ezekiel 6 Psalms 44
4	1 Samuel 28 1 Corinthians 9	Ezekiel 7 Psalms 45
5	1 Samuel 29, 30 1 Corinthians 10	Ezekiel 8 Psalms 46, 47

6	1 Samuel 31 1 Corinthians 11	Ezekiel 9 Psalms 48
7	2 Samuel 1 1 Corinthians 12	Ezekiel 10 Psalms 49
8	2 Samuel 2 1 Corinthians 13	Ezekiel 11 Psalms 50
9	2 Samuel 3 1 Corinthians 14	Ezekiel 12 Psalms 51
10	2 Samuel 4, 5 1 Corinthians 15	Ezekiel 13 Psalms 52–54
11	2 Samuel 6 1 Corinthians 16	Ezekiel 14 Psalms 55
12	2 Samuel 7 2 Corinthians 1	Ezekiel 15 Psalms 56, 57
13	2 Samuel 8, 9 2 Corinthians 2	Ezekiel 16 Psalms 58, 59
14	2 Samuel 10 2 Corinthians 3	Ezekiel 17 Psalms 60, 61
15	2 Samuel 11 2 Corinthians 4	Ezekiel 18 Psalms 62, 63
16	2 Samuel 12 2 Corinthians 5	Ezekiel 19 Psalms 64, 65
17	2 Samuel 13 2 Corinthians 6	Ezekiel 20 Psalms 66, 67
18	2 Samuel 14 2 Corinthians 7	Ezekiel 21 Psalms 68
19	2 Samuel 15 2 Corinthians 8	Ezekiel 22 Psalms 69
20	2 Samuel 16 2 Corinthians 9	Ezekiel 23 Psalms 70, 71
21	2 Samuel 17 2 Corinthians 10	Ezekiel 24 Psalms 72

22	2 Samuel 18 2 Corinthians 11	Ezekiel 25 Psalms 73
23	2 Samuel 19 2 Corinthians 12	Ezekiel 26 Psalms 74
24	2 Samuel 20 2 Corinthians 13	Ezekiel 27 Psalms 75, 76
25	2 Samuel 21 Galatians 1	Ezekiel 28 Psalms 77
26	2 Samuel 22 Galatians 2	Ezekiel 29 Psalms 78:1–37
27	2 Samuel 23 Galatians 3	Ezekiel 30 Psalms 78:38–72
28	2 Samuel 24 Galatians 4	Ezekiel 31 Psalms 79
29	1 Kings 1 Galatians 5	Ezekiel 32 Psalms 80
30	1 Kings 2 Galatians 6	Ezekiel 33 Psalms 81, 82

OCTOBER *"O how I love Thy law! It is my meditation all the day."*

Day	Family Reading	Secret Reading
1	1 Kings 3 Ephesians 1	Ezekiel 34 Psalms 83, 84
2	1 Kings 4, 5 Ephesians 2	Ezekiel 35 Psalms 85
3	1 Kings 6 Ephesians 3	Ezekiel 36 Psalms 86
4	1 Kings 7 Ephesians 4	Ezekiel 37 Psalms 87, 88
5	1 Kings 8 Ephesians 5	Ezekiel 38 Psalms 89

6	1 Kings 9 Ephesians 6	Ezekiel 39 Psalms 90
7	1 Kings 10 Philippians 1	Ezekiel 40 Psalms 91
8	1 Kings 11 Philippians 2	Ezekiel 41 Psalms 92, 93
9	1 Kings 12 Philippians 3	Ezekiel 42 Psalms 94
10	1 Kings 13 Philippians 4	Ezekiel 43 Psalms 95, 96
11	1 Kings 14 Colossians 1	Ezekiel 44 Psalms 97, 98
12	1 Kings 15 Colossians 2	Ezekiel 45 Psalms 99–101
13	1 Kings 16 Colossians 3	Ezekiel 46 Psalms 102
14	1 Kings 17 Colossians 4	Ezekiel 47 Psalms 103
15	1 Kings 18 1 Thess. 1	Ezekiel 48 Psalms 104
16	1 Kings 19 1 Thess. 2	Daniel 1 Psalms 105
17	1 Kings 20 1 Thess. 3	Daniel 2 Psalms 106
18	1 Kings 21 1 Thess. 4	Daniel 3 Psalms 107
19	1 Kings 22 1 Thess. 5	Daniel 4 Psalms 108, 109
20	2 Kings 1 2 Thess. 1	Daniel 5 Psalms 110, 111
21	2 Kings 2 2 Thess. 2	Daniel 6 Psalms 112, 113

22	2 Kings 3 2 Thess. 3	Daniel 7 Psalms 114, 115
23	2 Kings 4 1 Timothy 1	Daniel 8 Psalms 116
24	2 Kings 5 1 Timothy 2	Daniel 9 Psalms 117, 118
25	2 Kings 6 1 Timothy 3	Daniel 10 Psalms 119:1–24
26	2 Kings 7 1 Timothy 4	Daniel 11 Psalms 119:25–48
27	2 Kings 8 1 Timothy 5	Daniel 12 Psalms 119:49–72
28	2 Kings 9 1 Timothy 6	Hosea 1 Psalms 119:73–96
29	2 Kings 10 2 Timothy 1	Hosea 2 Psalms 119:97–120
30	2 Kings 11, 12 2 Timothy 2	Hosea 3, 4 Psalms 119:121–144
31	2 Kings 13 2 Timothy 3	Hosea 5, 6 Psalms 119:145–176

NOVEMBER *"As new-born babes, desire the sincere milk of the word, that ye may grow thereby."*

Day	Family Reading	Secret Reading
1	2 Kings 14 2 Timothy 4	Hosea 7 Psalms 120–122
2	2 Kings 15 Titus 1	Hosea 8 Psalms 123–125
3	2 Kings 16 Titus 2	Hosea 9 Psalms 126–128
4	2 Kings 17 Titus 3	Hosea 10 Psalms 129–131

5	2 Kings 18 Philemon 1	Hosea 11 Psalms 132–134
6	2 Kings 19 Hebrews 1	Hosea 12 Psalms 135, 136
7	2 Kings 20 Hebrews 2	Hosea 13 Psalms 137, 138
8	2 Kings 21 Hebrews 3	Hosea 14 Psalms 139
9	2 Kings 22 Hebrews 4	Joel 1 Psalms 140, 141
10	2 Kings 23 Hebrews 5	Joel 2 Psalms 142
11	2 Kings 24 Hebrews 6	Joel 3 Psalms 143
12	2 Kings 25 Hebrews 7	Amos 1 Psalms 144
13	1 Chron. 1, 2 Hebrews 8	Amos 2 Psalms 145
14	1 Chron. 3, 4 Hebrews 9	Amos 3 Psalms 146, 147
15	1 Chron. 5, 6 Hebrews 10	Amos 4 Psalms 148–150
16	1 Chron. 7, 8 Hebrews 11	Amos 5 Luke 1:1–38
17	1 Chron. 9, 10 Hebrews 12	Amos 6 Luke 1:39–80
18	1 Chron. 11, 12 Hebrews 13	Amos 7 Luke 2
19	1 Chron. 13, 14 James 1	Amos 8 Luke 3
20	1 Chron. 15 James 2	Amos 9 Luke 4

21	1 Chron. 16	Obadiah 1
	James 3	Luke 5
22	1 Chron. 17	Jonah 1
	James 4	Luke 6
23	1 Chron. 18	Jonah 2
	James 5	Luke 7
24	1 Chron. 19, 20	Jonah 3
	1 Peter 1	Luke 8
25	1 Chron. 21	Jonah 4
	1 Peter 2	Luke 9
26	1 Chron. 22	Micah 1
	1 Peter 3	Luke 10
27	1 Chron. 23	Micah 2
	1 Peter 4	Luke 11
28	1 Chron. 24, 25	Micah 3
	1 Peter 5	Luke 12
29	1 Chron. 26, 27	Micah 4
	2 Peter 1	Luke 13
30	1 Chron. 28	Micah 5
	2 Peter 2	Luke 14

DECEMBER *"The law of his God is in his heart; none of his steps shall slide."*

Day	Family Reading	Secret Reading
1	1 Chron. 29	Micah 6
	2 Peter 3	Luke 15
2	2 Chron. 1	Micah 7
	1 John 1	Luke 16
3	2 Chron. 2	Nahum 1
	1 John 2	Luke 17
4	2 Chron. 3, 4	Nahum 2
	1 John 3	Luke 18

5	2 Chron. 5, 6:1–11 1 John 4	Nahum 3 Luke 19
6	2 Chron. 6:12–42 1 John 5	Habakkuk 1 Luke 20
7	2 Chron. 7 2 John 1	Habakkuk 2 Luke 21
8	2 Chron. 8 3 John 1	Habakkuk 3 Luke 22
9	2 Chron. 9 Jude 1	Zephaniah 1 Luke 23
10	2 Chron. 10 Revelation 1	Zephaniah 2 Luke 24
11	2 Chron. 11, 12 Revelation 2	Zephaniah 3 John 1
12	2 Chron. 13 Revelation 3	Haggai 1 John 2
13	2 Chron. 14, 15 Revelation 4	Haggai 2 John 3
14	2 Chron. 16 Revelation 5	Zechariah 1 John 4
15	2 Chron. 17 Revelation 6	Zechariah 2 John 5
16	2 Chron. 18 Revelation 7	Zechariah 3 John 6
17	2 Chron. 19, 20 Revelation 8	Zechariah 4 John 7
18	2 Chron. 21 Revelation 9	Zechariah 5 John 8
19	2 Chron. 22, 23 Revelation 10	Zechariah 6 John 9
20	2 Chron. 24 Revelation 11	Zechariah 7 John 10

21	2 Chron. 25	Zechariah 8
	Revelation 12	John 11
22	2 Chron. 26	Zechariah 9
	Revelation 13	John 12
23	2 Chron. 27, 28	Zechariah 10
	Revelation 14	John 13
24	2 Chron. 29	Zechariah 11
	Revelation 15	John 14
25	2 Chron. 30	Zechariah 12, 13:1
	Revelation 16	John 15
26	2 Chron. 31	Zechariah 13:2–9
	Revelation 17	John 16
27	2 Chron. 32	Zechariah 14
	Revelation 18	John 17
28	2 Chron. 33	Malachi 1
	Revelation 19	John 18
29	2 Chron. 34	Malachi 2
	Revelation 20	John 19
30	2 Chron. 35	Malachi 3
	Revelation 21	John 20
31	2 Chron. 36	Malachi 4
	Revelation 22	John 21

Footnotes

1. A memorial account of Robert Murray McCheyne's life, written by friend and colleague Rev. J. Roxburgh in Andrew A. Bonar's book, *Memoir and Remains of the Reverend Robert Murray McCheyne* (1881 ed.), p. 593.

2. This quote, by Andrew A. Bonar, is found in his *Memoir and Remains of the Reverend Robert Murray McCheyne* (1881 ed.) p. 63.

3. Andrew A. Bonar, *Memoirs and Remains of the Reverend Robert Murray McCheyne* (1881 ed.), p. 562.

For more information on the life, ministry and writings of Robert Murray McCheyne see:

Andrew A. Bonar, *Memoir and Remains of the Reverend Robert Murray McCheyne* (1844).
Andrew A. Bonar, *Additional Remains of the Reverend Robert Murray McCheyne* (1846).
Andrew A. Bonar, *A Basket of Fragments* (1848).
Alexander Smellie, *Robert Murray McCheyne* (1913).
J. C. Smith, *Robert Murray McCheyne* (1910).
James A. Stewart, *Robert Murray McCheyne* (1963).